DECODABLE BOOK
BOOK 1-4

Harcourt
Orlando Boston Dallas Chicago San Diego
Visit *The Learning Site!*
www.hbschool.com

Printed in the United States of America

ISBN 0-15-320201-7

1 2 3 4 5 6 7 8 9 10 026 2002 01 00

Photo credits
Frans Lanting/Minden Pictures, 41; Frans Lanting/Minden Pictures, 42(both); Glen Allison/Tony Stone Images. 43; Art Wolfe/Tony Stone Images, 44; Stephen Krasemann/Tony Stone Images, 45; Merlin D. Tuttle, Bat Conservation International/Photo Researchers, 46, 47; Joe McDonald/Visuals Unlimited, 48.

Contents

Lee Needs Sleep

by Betsy Franco
illustrated by
Jennifer Beck Harris

Lee is sleeping under a big tree. He is dreaming of little green sheep.

Bee sees Lee sleeping.
Bee buzzes all around Lee.
Buzz, buzz. Buzz, buzz.

Bug sees Lee sleeping.
Bug creeps up Lee's leg.
Creep, creep. Creep, creep.

Flea sees Lee sleeping.
Flea hops on Lee.
Hop, leap. Hop, leap.

Buzz, buzz! Creep, creep!
Hop, leap! Lee is mad.
He can't sleep!

Lee starts thinking. What will he do? At last, Lee has a grand plan!

Bee, Bug, and Flea eat. Now Lee can sleep!

Wake Up, Blake

by Gail Williams
illustrated by C. D. Hullinger

"Wake up, Blake!" called Nate. "Let's go to Kate's cabin at the lake."

"I am glad you came," Kate said. "Let's skate." Kate and Nate started skating, but Blake did not skate.

Blake is sleeping on a crate! "Wake up, Blake!" called Kate. "Let's rake."

Kate and Nate made a big hill. Blake did not rake.

"Wake up, Blake!" called Kate.

"I didn't want to skate or rake," yelled Blake. "Let's all bake a cake!"

Kate and Nate did not bake. Blake baked his cake. Then Blake called, "Nate! Kate!"

"Wake up, Kate and Nate!" Blake giggled.

Benny Bunny

by Mary Hogan
illustrated by Holly Cooper

Benny Bunny is Patty's pet rabbit. Benny has fluffy black fur.

This bunny is a clean pet. Benny licks his fur — just like a cat.

Patty brushes Benny's fur.
Benny thinks that's
really neat.

Patty feeds Benny leafy greens and bits of apple. Benny thinks that's really neat.

Patty plays with Benny. He hops in and out of boxes. Benny thinks that's really neat.

If Benny is sleepy, Patty rubs his belly. Benny thinks that's really neat.

Benny lets Patty hug him.
Patty thinks that's
really neat!

Mike's Job

by Susan Blackaby
illustrated by Joe Cepeda

Mike has a job. He watches Miss Wise's pets. Miss Wise is off on a quick trip.

Mike gets cash for his job. That's a neat deal. Mike rides his bike up Pine Drive to Miss Wise's home.

A dog with black spots sits in the yard. It jumps up as Mike comes in the gate. "Well, dog, let's get inside."

Mike feeds the dog. Mike feeds the fish and the bird.

Miss Wise gets back and calls Mike. "Thanks for feeding the fish and the bird."

"I really like your dog, Miss Wise. It is sweet."

“Thanks, Mike,
but it isn’t mine!”

Wendy

by Sheila Black
illustrated by Richard Bernal

“It’s reading time. No whispering,” Miss Wheelman says. Wendy never whispers.

“No whirling and twirling at play time,” Miss Wheelman says. Wendy never whirls and twirls.

"No whipping up milk at snack time," Miss Wheelman says. Wendy never whips up her milk.

"No humming at rest time," Miss Wheelman says. Wendy never hums.

“No hogging all the white,” Miss Wheelman says.

Wendy never hogs things, but she needs lots and lots of white.

"Good job!" Miss Wheelman says as she winks at Wendy. Wendy just grins.

BATS

by Lisa deMauro

Bats are mammals that can fly. They have hands with fingers and feet.

Bats make homes in dark places. Bats sleep in caves, in attics, or in trees.

When the sun shines, bats sleep. Bats hang upside down when they are resting.

When the sun sets, bats wake up and hunt for bugs. City bats go past street lamps, hunting for bugs. Country bats dart into the forest, hunting for a meal.

Bats can help us. They eat a lot of bugs. Bats eat bugs that hurt farm crops. Bats eat bugs that bite us, too!

Bats even help plants grow.

That makes them twice as nice!

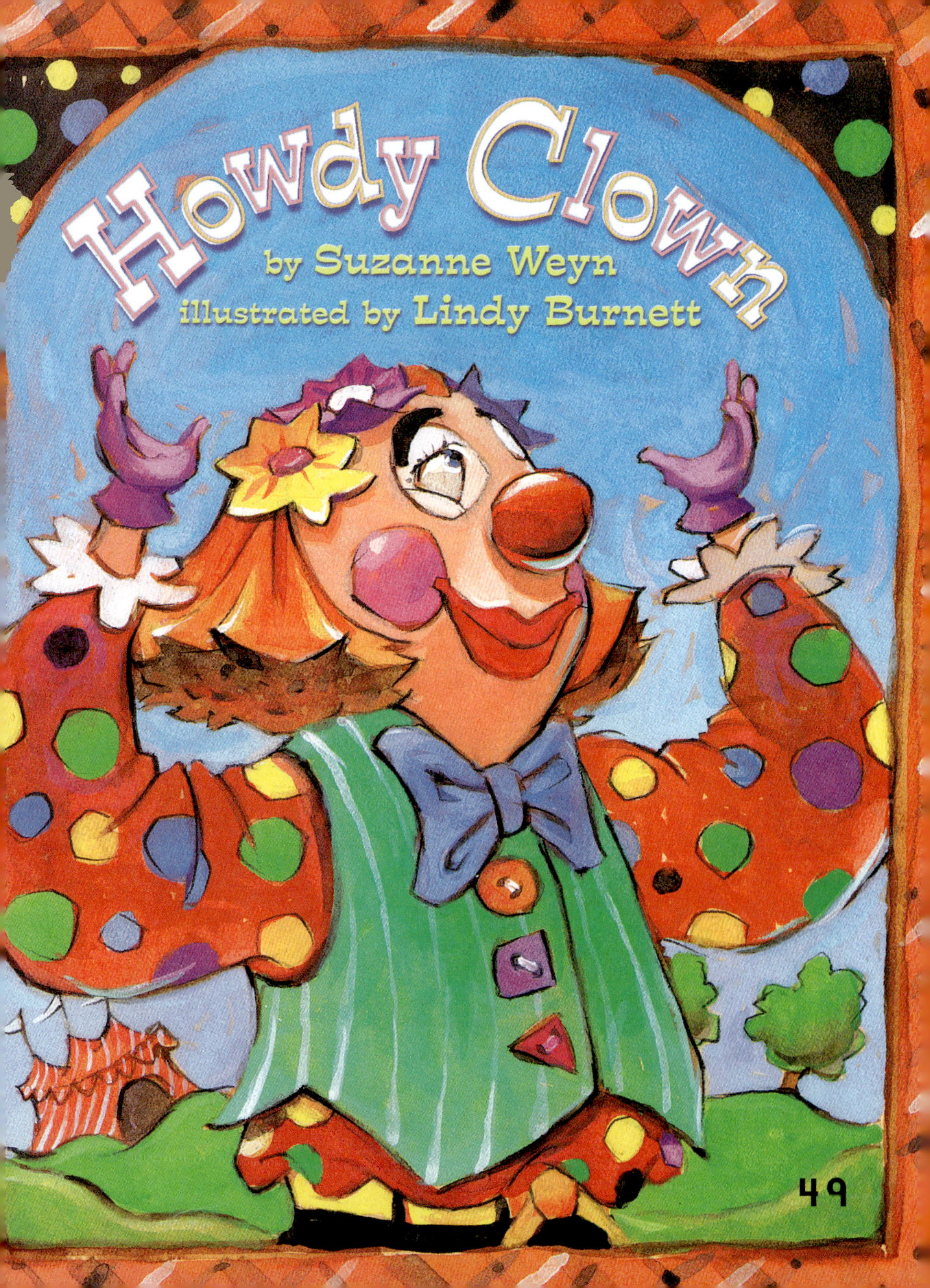
Howdy Clown
by Suzanne Weyn
illustrated by Lindy Burnett

Howdy Clown trots into town.
She looks up.
She looks down.

She looks up
and sees a smile.
It makes her giggle
all the while.

She looks down
and sees red lips.
"Wow! Just what I need!"
Howdy yips.

She slaps the lips
on her face.
She frowns and growls
all over the place!

Now Howdy Clown
is feeling sad.
Now Howdy Clown
is feeling bad.

She flips her lips
upside down.

Now Howdy has a smile —
not a frown!

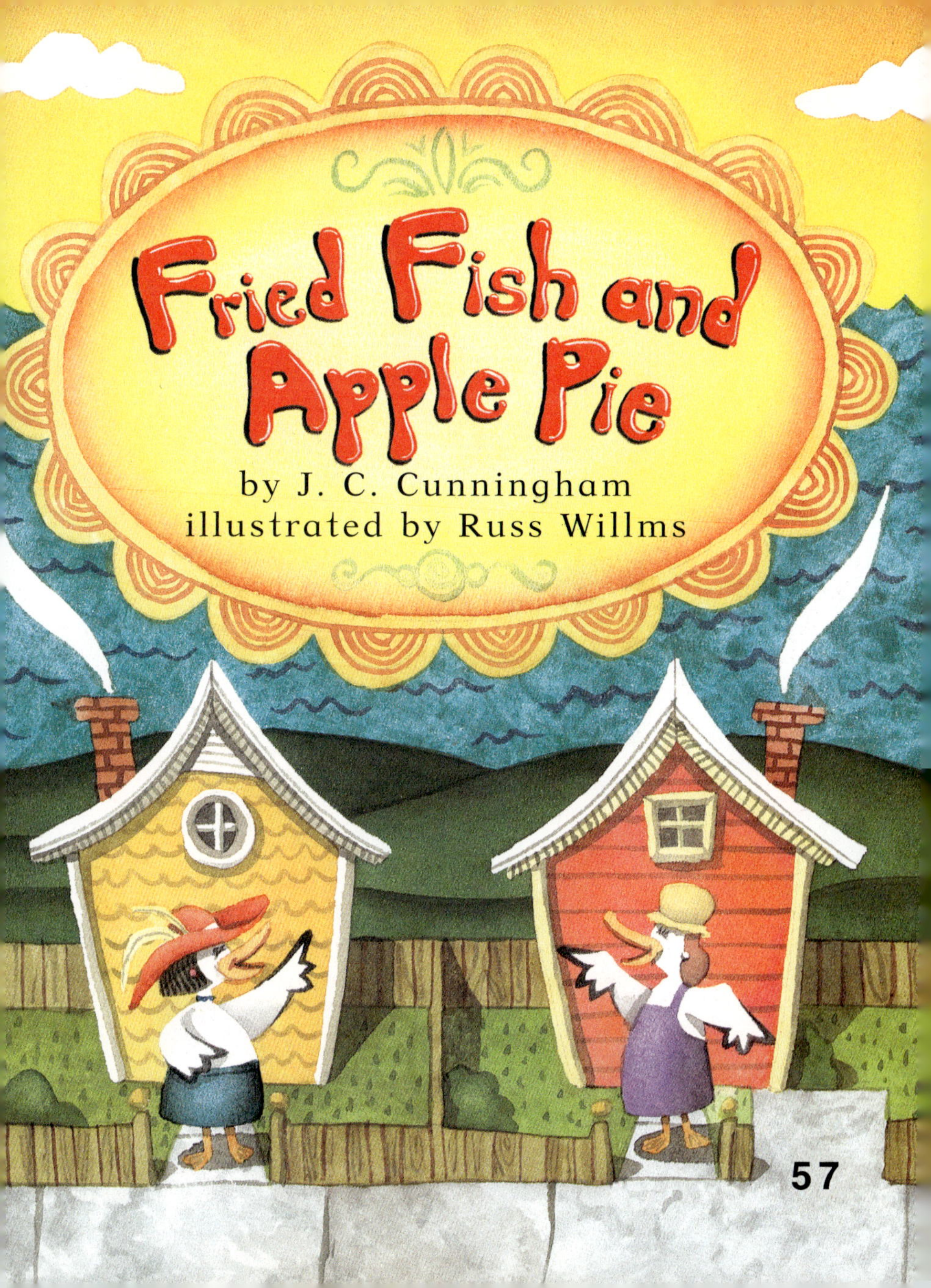

Fried Fish and Apple Pie

by J. C. Cunningham

illustrated by Russ Willms

Kathy made the best fried fish. Betty made the best apple pie.

Kathy had a plan. "Let's sell our fried fish and apple pie!" cried Kathy.

Kathy and Betty set up a stand by the beach. "Try my fried fish!" honked Kathy.

"Try my fresh apple pie!" honked Betty. Kathy and Betty didn't sell a thing!

Betty had a plan. “Let’s try the sky!” she cried. “Flying Freddy can help us!”

Kathy and Betty made a big banner and tied it to Freddy's plane.

"Thanks, Freddy!" cried Kathy and Betty.

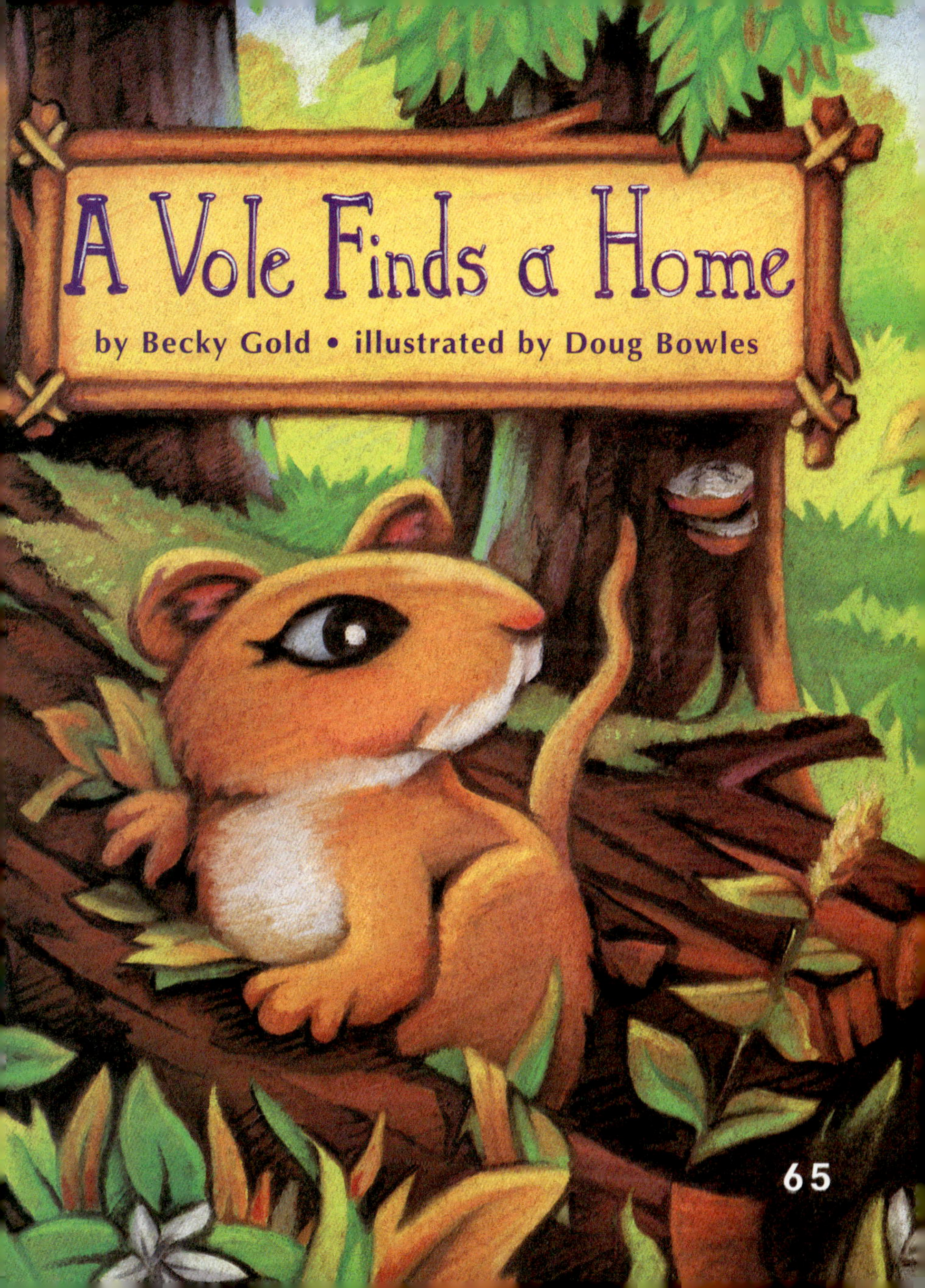

A Vole Finds a Home

by Becky Gold • illustrated by Doug Bowles

What is this animal? It's a vole. Voles are field mice.

Voles make nests in holes. This vole pokes its nose out of its home.

What is a vole's home like?
It's crowded! Space is close.

When a vole grows up, it's time to make its own nest.

This vole is looking for a home. It stops to eat. Voles like seeds.

The vole pokes its nose in a hole. It digs past a stone and wiggles in.

Sniff, sniff. What's that?
Another vole! How nice!